Contents

What is suicide?

Growing up can be a difficult time. Although most people sail through their teenage years with few worries, some find it harder to cope. Problems such as exams, bullying or constant arguments with someone close may make them feel angry, stressed or frightened. In a few cases, people may feel so bad they even end up committing suicide. Deep down inside, they usually do not really want to die. But death may look like the only way of stopping what seems like endless misery.

Famous suicides

Feeling so unhappy that you think about killing yourself is nothing new. All sorts of people, including the rich and famous, may be struck by suicidal feelings. The Egyptian queen, Cleopatra, for example, allowed herself to be bitten by a poisonous snake more than two thousand years ago.

Kurt Cobain, singer with the grunge band Nirvana, battled with depression and a drug habit for many years before finally taking his own life in 1994.

Need to Know

Teenage Suicide

Claire Wallerstein

Heinemann
LIBRARY

www.heinemann.co.uk/library

Visit our website to find out more information about **Heinemann Library** books.

To order:

☎ Phone 44 (0) 1865 888066

📄 Send a fax to 44 (0) 1865 314091

💻 Visit the Heinemann Bookshop at www.heinemann.co.uk/library to browse our catalogue and order online.

Produced by Roger Coote Publishing
Gissing's Farm, Fressingfield, Suffolk IP21 5SH, UK

First published in Great Britain by Heinemann Library, Halley Court, Jordan Hill, Oxford OX2 8EJ, part of Harcourt Education.
Heinemann is a registered trademark of Harcourt Education Ltd.

Editorial: Cath Senker
Design: Jane Hawkins
Picture Research: Lynda Lines
Consultant: Christina Thompson
Production: Viv Hichens

Originated by Ambassador Litho Ltd
Printed and bound in China by South China Printing Company

ISBN 0 431 09820 4
07 06 05 04 03
10 9 8 7 6 5 4 3 2 1

British Library Cataloguing in Publication Data
Wallerstein, Claire
    Teenage suicide. - (Need to know)
    1.Suicide - Juvenile literature 2.Teenagers - Suicidal behaviour - Juvenile literature
    I.Title
    362.2'8'0835

Acknowledgements
The publishers would like to thank the following for permission to reproduce photographs:
Ancient Art and Architecture p. 7; Associated Press p. 33 (Detroit Free Press); Corbis pp. 5 (Stockmarket), 10 (Michael Lewis), 17 (Stockmarket/Gary D. Landsman), 50 (Stockmarket/ Mug Shots); Digital Vision p. 35; Getty Images *front cover* main image (Chris Baker); Hodder Wayland Picture Library pp. 37, 40 (APM Studios), 49 (Angela Hampton); John Birdsall p.19; Panos p. 48 (Giacoma Pirozzi); Peter Newark p. 9; Popperfoto pp. 4 (Bettman/Reuters), 18 (Reuters/Gregg Newto), 30 (Reuters), 45; Rex Features pp. 13 (Brendan Beirne), 15 (Phanie Agency), 21 (Nina Berman), 22 (David Allocca), 23 (Tim Rooke), 26, 39 (Phil Rees), 47 (Ray Tang); Science Photo Library p. 34 (Annabella Bluesky); Topham Picturepoint pp. 11, 14, 25 (The Image Works), 28, 29 (PressNet), 32 (The Image Works/Kathy McLaughlin), 36 (The Image Works), 42 (Novosti), 43.

Every effort has been made to contact copyright holders of any material reproduced in this book. Any omissions will be rectified in subsequent printings if notice is given to the publishers.

Any words appearing in the text in bold, **like this**, are explained in the Glossary.

More recently, the rock star Kurt Cobain took his own life in the 1990s. Suicide is strongly linked to **depression**. Sadly, however, many suicidal people do not even realize that they are suffering from this common medical condition. It can usually be successfully treated.

The suicide rate

Today at least one per cent of all deaths around the world is from suicide. In 2000, around one million people died from suicide. That means one person killed themselves every 40 seconds. In the USA suicide kills twice as many people as AIDS. The suicide rate among adults has been rising quite slowly in most countries. But the picture is very different among the young, and especially among young men. The suicide rate among people aged 15 to 24 in most **industrialized countries** has tripled or even quadrupled since 1960.

This means youth suicide is now a major cause of concern for governments and doctors. Yet they are still far from understanding all of the reasons behind this massive increase. This is partly because many adults still find it hard to accept or understand that young people could want to kill themselves.

❝The world was so dark, it seemed the sun never came out. When I picture that time in my mind, it is always darkness.❞

(Anonymous US teenager who attempted suicide, discussing her feelings on a web page)

Suicide in history

The way in which we think about suicide has changed greatly throughout human history. In the past, many people mistakenly saw it as a heroic thing to do. In Ancient Greece and Rome, for example, people did not think the way they died was important, as long as it was with honour. Criminals were often offered the choice of suicide as an alternative to execution. Similarly, the Scandinavian Vikings believed that warriors who died in battle would receive the greatest honours for bravery in the afterlife – closely followed by those who committed suicide.

The sin of suicide

In the early days of Christianity, suicide was common among some strict religious groups. The Donatists wanted to get to heaven as soon as possible without waiting for a natural death. They were famous for throwing themselves off cliffs in huge numbers, or paying complete strangers to kill them.

By the 6th century, church leaders were so worried by the number of deaths that they declared suicide a sin. A person who committed suicide was buried at a crossroads. A stake was driven through his or her heart. It was believed the person could not enter heaven without a Christian burial. People who tried to kill themselves, but failed, were executed. This practice continued, in countries such as England, until the 19th century. In 1993, Ireland became the last country in Europe to get rid of the old laws declaring suicide a crime.

Other religious views

Other major religions look harshly on suicide too. According to Islam, people who commit suicide are condemned to hell, as only Allah (God) can say when we should die. One big exception is jihad, a 'holy war' to protect Islam. In this case, people who commit suicide believe they will become martyrs, and that Allah will reward them with great gifts in heaven. A group of terrorists who claimed to be fighting such a jihad killed themselves, along with over 3000 innocent people, during the attacks in New York and Washington, DC in September 2001. Most Muslims disagree strongly with such extreme acts of violence, however.

According to Orthodox Jewish teachings, suicide is as bad as murder, except in some extreme cases.

For example, in 73 CE, 960 Jews on the clifftop of Masada, Judaea faced capture by the Romans after a long siege. Instead they committed mass suicide by jumping to their deaths.

People of many Eastern religions, such as Buddhism and Shintoism, believe in reincarnation – the rebirth of the soul in another body. This means that suicide is not viewed so sternly.

A certain type of ritual suicide called suttee was actually expected of Hindu women in India and only banned in 1829. If her husband died, the woman was supposed to throw herself on his funeral pyre (the bonfire burning his body) to show her grief.

A Roman falls on his sword in this ancient carving. For people who lived in a violent age when many people died young, suicide was seen as a dignified death.

Religious cults

Sometimes, people have committed mass suicide after being brainwashed by religious **cults**. In 2000, hundreds of members of a cult in Uganda locked themselves in a church and set it alight. They had been told the end of the world was coming.

Protest suicides

Some people use suicide as a drastic means of protest when they feel there are no other options. For example, Thich Quang Duc, a Buddhist monk, set fire to himself in the Vietnamese city of Saigon in 1963. He wanted to protest against the government's bad treatment of Buddhists.

Hara-kiri

In other cases, suicide has been seen as a matter of dignity. In Japan, for example, a type of suicide called **hara-kiri** developed in the 16th century. It involved a very elaborate ceremony. The person committing hara-kiri, which means 'belly slit', had to **disembowel** himself – pull out his intestines – with a dagger. Then an assistant would chop off his head.

The last well-known person to commit hara-kiri was the writer, Yukio Mishima, in 1970.

Today, suicide may still be expected in a few **hunter-gatherer societies**. Living in rainforests and other wild places, people survive by hunting animals and gathering fruits and vegetables. Because they do not farm crops, it can sometimes be difficult to find enough food. Old and sick people, who can no longer help provide for the group, may be expected to kill themselves if supplies run low.

"Death is before me today. Like the recovery of a sick man...like the longing of a man to see his home again after many years of captivity."

(The earliest known discussion of suicide, in a fragment of Ancient Egyptian writing dating back to 2100 BCE)

A Japanese samurai warrior prepares to thrust a dagger into his stomach as he commits *hara-kiri*, viewed as the ultimate act of honour and bravery.

Who commits suicide?

People in some countries are more likely to commit suicide than in others. For example, rates are very high in the former Soviet republics. There, people have had to cope with high unemployment and other problems since the collapse of the Communist system in 1991. Developing countries seem to have much lower rates. This may be because many people lead more traditional lifestyles than in the West, and may have stronger family relationships. It probably also has a lot to do with the authorities failing to keep good records about what people have died from.

People in some professions, such as vets, are more likely to commit suicide than others.

Countries colonized relatively recently, such as the USA, Canada, Australia and New Zealand, have high rates of suicide. This may be because people do not have the same shared history and sense of belonging that exists in older countries.

Factors in suicide

Ethnicity can also have an effect. In the United States, for example, the suicide rate is highest among white people. However, the number of black and Hispanic people committing suicide is rising fast – especially among the young. Suicide rates among black children aged ten to fourteen rose almost 300 per cent between 1980 and 2000.

People of certain professions, such as vets, dentists, doctors and farmers, are particularly likely to commit suicide. On top of their stressful jobs, it is easy for them to get hold of guns, pesticides or dangerous drugs. Vets and farmers often destroy sick or 'useless' animals. They may see this as the best option for themselves if they feel they too are 'useless'.

Age is important too. The highest suicide rate is among the elderly, especially white men over the age of 75. They often suffer from serious illnesses or are put into nursing homes, which may make them feel lonely and depressed. However, most suicides, in terms of actual numbers, happen among the young. In the USA it is the third leading cause of death among 15 to 24-year-olds.

Gender also plays a role. Women and girls are more likely to suffer from **depression** than men, and are around three times more likely to try to commit suicide. Yet about six times more males than females actually succeed in killing themselves. This is because they tend to use more violent methods. Girls are more likely to take drug overdoses, which can often be treated in hospital.

Religion could be a factor. In places where suicide is forbidden, such as Muslim countries, it seems not to exist. But this could be because embarrassed families say the death was from another cause. In Europe, there are usually lower rates in Catholic countries than Protestant ones, which take a milder view of suicide. However, Catholic Hungary has one of the highest suicide rates in the world.

Who commits suicide?

Family links

There are certain patterns to suicide. Writing in the late 1800s, the French **sociologist** Émile Durkheim blamed the Industrial Revolution for the rapid rise in suicide. As people moved from villages in the countryside to cities, religion, tradition and family links were broken down. He said this could lead to **depression** and suicidal urges.

This still seems to hold true today. People without strong social or family contacts, such as single, divorced and widowed people, have a higher than average risk of committing suicide. There are more suicides at certain times, such as at the beginning of the week and during holidays – especially Christmas and Valentine's Day. At these times depressed people may feel lonelier than ever. Most teenagers kill themselves at home in the afternoon or early evening.

Many Aborigines have lost their traditional way of life and survive in miserable conditions at the edges of society in Australia – one of the world's richest countries.

"The pace of life is faster than ever now. There is academic pressure, peer group pressure to get involved in things like drugs, pressure to find a good job and, for young men especially, our society still expects them to have a stiff upper lip."

(Samaritans chief executive Simon Armson)

Loss of culture

In Australia, the rate of suicide among young **Aborigines** – once almost unheard of – is four times higher than among the general population. A 1994 study suggested that these high rates stem from Aboriginal people being forced out of their ancestral lands by white settlers and losing their traditional culture. They have often not been able to adjust to modern life. Aborigines suffer high rates of unemployment and poverty. These in turn can lead to higher rates of alcoholism, drug abuse, family violence and sexual abuse. All of these are risk factors for suicide. The situation is even worse among **indigenous** youths in North America, while in New Zealand the government has set up a special suicide prevention programme for young **Maoris**.

Suicide hotspots

Japan

In Japan, suicide has traditionally been seen as an honourable way of dying. For example, **kamikaze** pilots in the Second World War felt proud to crash their aeroplanes into enemy targets. In recent years, a major economic slump in Japan has led to many people, especially middle-aged men, taking their own lives after losing their jobs or being unable to pay off debts.

A DIY guide, *The Perfect Suicide Manual*, was in the bestseller lists for years until it was banned. There are several suicide websites too. A wood on the slopes of Mount Fuji near Tokyo has attracted many suicidal people. In 1998 alone, 70 bodies were found in the forest. The local authorities then put up signs saying: 'Think of the pain you will cause your family before you take any drastic action.'

Thousands of young Japanese air pilots, like the one in this plane about to crash into the USS *Missouri* in 1945, killed themselves trying to destroy enemy ships. Kamikaze means 'divine wind'.

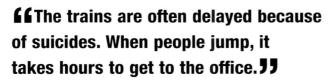

❝The trains are often delayed because of suicides. When people jump, it takes hours to get to the office.❞

(Female commuter travelling on the so-called 'suicide line' railway in western Tokyo, where many people have taken their own lives)

Finland

One of the reasons behind the high rate of suicide in Finland could be a kind of **depression** called **seasonal affective disorder** (SAD). It is caused by the lack of ultra-violet light found in sunshine. During the long, dark months of the Scandinavian winter, the Sun only rises above the horizon for a couple of hours each day. SAD symptoms include feelings of despair, depression, disrupted sleep and lack of energy. SAD is most common in women and can affect people in any country with low levels of winter sunlight. There are an estimated 10 million sufferers in the northern United States.

SAD can usually be helped with **phototherapy**, a treatment with bright ultra-violet lamps. This is offered by the medical services in Scandinavian countries. Many cafés also have the lamps. Finland has a very high rate of alcohol abuse, another risk factor in suicide.

Phototherapy lamps work by mimicking the Sun's rays, 'tricking' a person's body into thinking that winter has already passed.

Explosion in youth suicide

In the USA, twelve young people kill themselves each day. One teenager in every three now knows someone who has attempted suicide. The picture in Canada is similar. It is even worse in Australia and New Zealand, where only traffic accidents cause more youth deaths.

And the figures may be even higher than we think. In some countries, such as the UK, coroners (the officials who carry out inquiries after deaths) can record a verdict of suicide only if suicide is proved 'beyond all reasonable doubt'. This means that some car accidents involving only one vehicle are recorded as accidental deaths, but may actually be suicide. Similarly, some drug overdoses may be suicides.

Depression

In some surveys, around half of young people in Western countries say they suffer from loneliness and **depression** from time to time. Doctors do not fully understand why depression seems to be rising so fast, but point out that only a very few depressed people will actually kill themselves.

Although girls are still the most likely to attempt suicide, the rate of suicide is actually going up much faster among boys than girls. This is mainly because they use more violent methods. It may also be because many traditionally 'male' jobs in farming, fishing or manufacturing have disappeared. This can make some boys feel hopeless about their future.

It can also be harder for boys to seek help than girls. They may bottle up their feelings and might turn to drink or drugs for comfort. In a 2001 survey by the Samaritans, 20 per cent of young people said they would laugh if a male friend told them he was depressed.

School days are the best days of a person's life, or so the old saying goes. But more and more young people these days feel under enormous pressure, and a very few choose a violent and drastic solution to their problems.

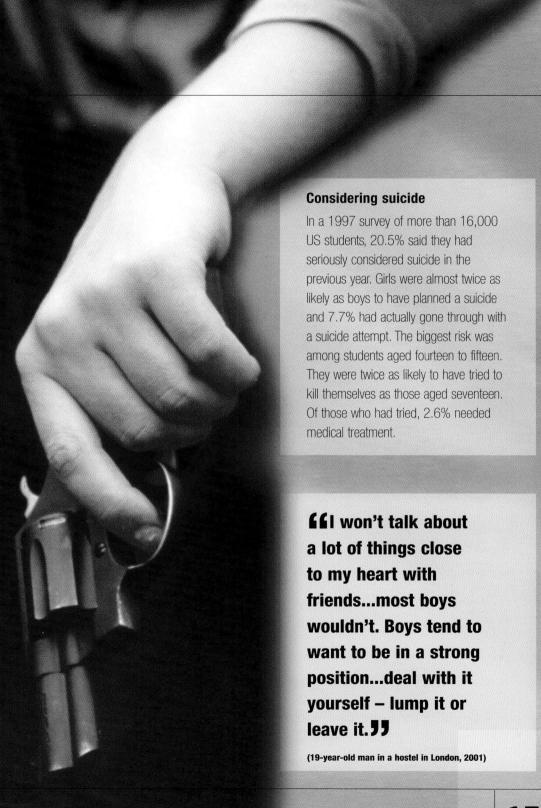

Considering suicide

In a 1997 survey of more than 16,000 US students, 20.5% said they had seriously considered suicide in the previous year. Girls were almost twice as likely as boys to have planned a suicide and 7.7% had actually gone through with a suicide attempt. The biggest risk was among students aged fourteen to fifteen. They were twice as likely to have tried to kill themselves as those aged seventeen. Of those who had tried, 2.6% needed medical treatment.

ＣＣI won't talk about a lot of things close to my heart with friends...most boys wouldn't. Boys tend to want to be in a strong position...deal with it yourself – lump it or leave it.ＪＪ

(19-year-old man in a hostel in London, 2001)

Teenagers at risk

Nearly everyone who is suicidal is depressed. **Depression** may be caused by something obvious, such as suffering from abuse or a parent dying. Often it has no clear reason at all. It can make people feel utterly miserable, as if a black cloud is hanging over them which is never going to disappear. Very few depressed people actually kill themselves. However, other problems in their lives can sometimes act like a trigger, pushing them to thoughts of suicide.

Homelessness

For example, homeless children have a high risk of committing suicide. Many teenagers living rough have run away from problems at home such as sexual or physical abuse, or big arguments with parents or step-parents. They may become victims of violence or abuse from other people living on the streets. This can deepen their anxiety and depression.

Drink and drugs

Many teens use drink or drugs to help them forget about their problems. However, alcohol and drugs can make depression worse and affect a person's ability to think straight. One young person in every three who commits suicide is drunk or on drugs.

Homeless people, such as these people sleeping rough in Brazil, have a stressful and uncertain life. They are at the mercy of the weather and may be moved on by police or beaten up by criminals.

❝We used to hear of suicides on the news, but now they're so common they aren't reported.❞

(Anonymous fifteen-year-old interviewed about youth suicide by the Scout Association of Australia)

Some bullies physically attack people. Others tease and pick on their victims all the time, making them feel lonely, frightened and depressed. Very occasionally it is so bad that death seems like the only way out.

Problems at school

Other children who may become suicidal are perfectionists or over-achievers at school. Their parents, or they themselves, may set extremely high standards. They may not be able to cope with the pressure. Some may be victims of bullying. There is at least one bullying-related suicide, or '**bullycide**', each month in the UK alone. The youngest victim was only eight years old. More than one-third of children experience bullying at some point.

Risk factors for suicide include:

- Breaking up with a girlfriend/boyfriend or having had an **abortion**.
- Being in prison. It can be difficult and frightening to cope with being locked up for a long period of time, sometimes with older, hardened criminals.
- Homosexuality. Teenagers coming to terms with being gay are ten times more likely to commit suicide than others their age. They may feel under pressure to 'live a lie', keeping their sexuality secret from friends and family.

Underlying causes

Nearly all people who kill themselves have some kind of common mental illness, usually **depression**. Having such an illness does not make a person 'mad' though. In fact, at least one in four of us will suffer from depression at some stage in our lives. It is often because the chemicals in our brains have got slightly out of balance. Sometimes depression creeps up so slowly that people do not realize anything is wrong. They think it is normal to always feel miserable.

Mental illness

Although most people who commit suicide are depressed, it is important to remember that very few depressed people actually commit suicide. In fact, many of today's most successful celebrities and role models suffer from depression. As well as depression (also called **unipolar affective disorder**), other less common problems linked to suicide also often start to appear in the teenage years. These are **manic depression (bipolar affective disorder)**, **schizophrenia**, eating disorders, alcoholism and drug abuse.

Illnesses such as depression can make people less able to cope with difficulties, such as important exams and relationship problems.

Finding it hard to cope with problems has nothing to do with intelligence, but rather a person's way of seeing the world. Some people may see a stressful event as an exciting challenge, but it might make a depressed person feel totally desperate. Mental illness sufferers are between five and fifteen times more likely to commit suicide than the population as a whole. With schizophrenia, a voice may actually command the person to kill him or herself even though that person does not want to die.

Successful treatment

The good news is that these illnesses can usually be successfully treated. But some young people are too frightened or embarrassed to ask for help. While 90 per cent of young people who kill themselves have some kind of mental illness, only 15 per cent are actually having treatment at the time of their death.

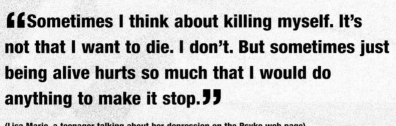

❝Sometimes I think about killing myself. It's not that I want to die. I don't. But sometimes just being alive hurts so much that I would do anything to make it stop.❞

(Lisa Marie, a teenager talking about her depression on the Psyke web page)

Anorexics have a kind of mental illness which makes them obsessed with dieting and controlling their body weight, even when they are dangerously thin. Many anorexics suffer from depression.

Guide to mental illnesses

We now know that getting a mental illness is no more someone's fault than catching a cold. It is no good telling depressed people to 'snap out of it'. Mental illnesses are usually caused by a real problem with a person's brain chemistry, which can be treated. These are some of the most common illnesses.

Depression

Although many people suffer from **depression** at some stage, for some people it has no obvious cause and cannot be shaken off. Even young children can suffer from depression. Famous sufferers include Fiona Apple, Marlon Brando, Jim Carrey, Queen Elizabeth II, Elton John, Janet Jackson, Alanis Morissette and Winona Ryder.

Eating disorders

People with eating disorders become completely obsessed with their weight. **Anorexics** starve themselves – sometimes to the point of death.

The US singer Fiona Apple takes regular medication for depression, and says her illness has been the inspiration behind her music.

Princess Diana was one of the world's richest and most glamorous women, loved by millions. Yet she was plagued by bulimia and depression.

Depression diagnosis

To be diagnosed with depression, a person will have at least five of the following symptoms for at least two weeks, on top of feeling continuously low:

- inability to sleep or sleeping too much
- appetite change, weight loss or gain
- mental and physical slowness
- inability to concentrate or make decisions
- loss of energy
- feeling worthless or guilty
- frequent thoughts of death or suicide.

Those suffering from **bulimia** will binge on food and then get rid of it by taking **laxatives** or making themselves vomit.

Manic depression

People with **manic depression** experience huge mood swings, ranging from a desperate low to an elated high, or mania. In manic periods, the person may be **hyperactive** (very energetic), be very busy and not need much sleep. About one per cent of the population suffers from this condition at some point. Some famous sufferers include Jean-Claude van Damme, Francis Ford Coppola, Robert Downey Jr., Axl Rose and Darryl Strawberry.

Schizophrenia

The rare condition **schizophrenia** has a wide range of symptoms, known as **psychosis**. People become unable to tell the difference between what is real and unreal. Paranoid schizophrenics may suffer **hallucinations** and **delusions**. They may become convinced that someone is spying on them, or trying to kill them. Disorganized schizophrenics may talk nonsense. They may be **catatonic** – rigid and hardly moving – or hyperactive. Schizophrenics may find it hard to make friends or keep a job.

High-risk families?

While scientists do not believe there is a 'suicide gene', people in some families do seem to have a higher than average risk of committing suicide. It seems faulty genes are passed on from generation to generation. These cause chemical imbalances in the brain and can lead to **depression**, and occasionally, to suicide. The risk of depression can be up to 70 per cent if a person's identical twin (who is genetically identical) also suffers from it. This occurs even if the twins were adopted and grew up in different families. **Manic depression**, **schizophrenia** and eating disorders also have a genetic link. The **genetic** link means that scientists may one day be able to cure some depressive illnesses. Using **gene therapy**, they hope to be able to remove or correct the damaged genes.

However, many other factors are involved. Eating disorders, for example, were rare 100 years ago, and so cannot be blamed on genetics alone. In fact, the glorification of very thin supermodels seems to have played a bigger role.

A gloomy outlook?

Children of depressed parents may learn by example to have a gloomy outlook on life. It is also possible that some family suicide clusters happen simply because the traumatic death of a child or close relative can make life seem unbearable, even for people who never felt

A genetic factor may mean some of these partygoers could get hooked on alcohol more easily than others. If they are depressed, alcohol could make things worse.

depressed beforehand. So it is important to remember that no one is 'doomed' to commit suicide. The genetic link simply means some people may have a greater tendency to do so.

Suicide is very complex, and people do not commit suicide just because of one particular feeling or problem.

Serotonin

Scientists at the Royal Ottawa Hospital in Canada have found that **DNA** (genetic material) from most suicidal patients has a mutation which healthy people do not have. This affects production of **serotonin**, a chemical in the brain that controls mood. In other experiments, rats killed their own babies when serotonin levels in their brains were lowered.

Parasuicide

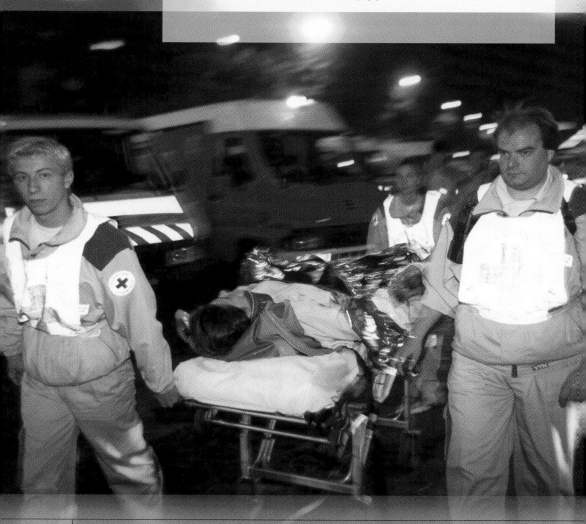

"I want to kill myself, but I don't want to be dead. I mean, I want to be dead, but I don't want to be dead for ever. I only want to be dead until my eighteenth birthday."

(Anonymous fifteen-year-old quoted on a web page)

Parasuicide is when people make a suicide attempt, but do not actually want to kill themselves. It is sometimes called **deliberate self-harm**. Usually, they take an overdose and then call a friend or the emergency services. Or they may carry out the act in a place where they hope to be found and helped. Sadly, this does not always happen. Help may not arrive until it is too late.

Parasuicide is not the same as when people deliberately harm themselves in less serious ways. For example, some people may cut themselves when they feel very stressed or upset. This is not life-threatening, and they do it because the pain somehow helps them.

A call for help

Parasuicide is usually a 'cry for help' from people, usually girls, who have trouble coping with their problems. They suffer from the same kind of difficulties as those who actually do commit suicide. They may feel it is the

People who commit parasuicide – like this French woman who drove her car into a crowd of football supporters – may do so to show how much they are hurting inside.

only way to make the people around them understand how bad, or how angry they are feeling. Some teenagers commit parasuicide because they want to frighten someone who has upset them and 'make them sorry'. This is very dangerous because some parasuicides end in death.

Parasuicide also shows how confused many suicidal young people are. They may want to take drastic action or even kill themselves, but often change their minds quite quickly. Few people are 100 per cent certain that they want to die. Even when they feel at their worst, there is nearly always a part of them that clings to life.

People who commit parasuicide may be told they are attention-seekers or time-wasters. Their families may be very angry and upset, making the person feel even more miserable and guilty. However, people who have committed parasuicide should be taken seriously. They are likely to try it again, and are up to twenty times more likely than the general population to finally take their own lives.

Copycat suicides

It is thought that one young person in every twenty who commits suicide could be copying the death or suicide of someone else, often an idol such as a pop or movie star. In one famous case in 1933, Kiyoko Matsumoto, a nineteen-year-old student, dramatically threw himself into a 330-metre deep volcanic crater on Oshima island in Japan. In the following months, 300 other teenagers did the same thing at the same place.

Most young people spend time fantasizing. They may be told they are always daydreaming, or 'have their head in the clouds'. Some identify so strongly with a person – often a pop star they have never met – that life may seem impossible without that person if he or she dies. Hollywood movies often glorify the idea of 'living fast, dying young' as a rebel rather than growing old and boring, and 'fading away'.

For some young people, the early deaths of talented or beautiful people, such as Marilyn Monroe, film star James Dean, 1960s rock star Jimi Hendrix (pictured left) and Nirvana singer Kurt Cobain, can seem romantically tragic. Many copycat suicides are among people of the same sex or age as the person being imitated. Copycats particularly seem to identify with the person if the death is portrayed as 'senseless' or the 'inexplicable act of a healthy person', which has left everyone baffled.

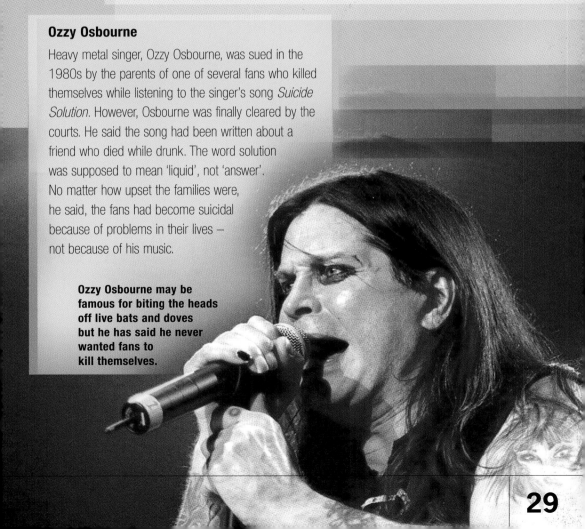

> **"Most people, in committing a suicidal act, are just as muddled as when they do anything important under emotional stress. Carefully planned acts of suicide are as rare as carefully planned acts of homicide [murder]."**
>
> (Erwin Stengel, suicide investigator, UK)

Ozzy Osbourne

Heavy metal singer, Ozzy Osbourne, was sued in the 1980s by the parents of one of several fans who killed themselves while listening to the singer's song *Suicide Solution*. However, Osbourne was finally cleared by the courts. He said the song had been written about a friend who died while drunk. The word solution was supposed to mean 'liquid', not 'answer'. No matter how upset the families were, he said, the fans had become suicidal because of problems in their lives — not because of his music.

Ozzy Osbourne may be famous for biting the heads off live bats and doves but he has said he never wanted fans to kill themselves.

The role of the media

Many researchers believe that high-profile news reports of deaths may push vulnerable or depressed people to commit copycat suicides. In one year in the 1970s, for example, there were 60 suicides by burning in the UK after reports of a woman burning herself to death in Switzerland. Such suicides are normally extremely rare.

These deaths create a problem for journalists. Dramatic suicides are worth reporting. They usually interest readers a lot more than boring stories about parliamentary politics. So suicide prevention organizations are trying to teach journalists to write about them more sensitively.

The way in which the media portray suicide can have a huge effect on some depressed or vulnerable people.

For example, when newspapers stopped their sensational reporting of suicides on the subway in Vienna, Austria, the number of such suicides fell from thirteen in 1986 to just three in 1989.

Spare us the details

The United Nations published reporting guidelines in 1996, advising the media not to focus on the hopelessness of the dead person's life or make suicide seem glamorous. They were told not to endlessly repeat the story or describe the method used. However, there is still a long way to go. In July 2001, the *New York Post* was criticized for a front-page story with the headline: 'Model found dead in pool of blood'. It went into great detail about how the woman had killed herself.

TV dramas

The stories in television dramas can have an important influence on young people. They send out dangerous signals if a child's suicide is shown to have a positive result, such as shaming school bullies. However, hospital dramas such as ER can be useful. For example, they can teach young people about the dangers of overdosing on painkillers.

Kurt Cobain

Suicide experts expected a big wave of copycat suicides after the star of the band Nirvana, Kurt Cobain, killed himself in 1994. However, there were actually very few. This may have been due to the sensitive and low-key media reports and the publication of helpline telephone numbers in the press. Thousands of young people did call these helplines to talk to counsellors in the weeks following Cobain's death. It seems they got over their grief by talking about it rather than actually ending their lives.

Euthanasia

The word **euthanasia** means 'good death' in Greek. Most euthanasia is carried out for people who are **terminally ill** with diseases such as cancer. They want to die before they start to suffer great pain, lose their mental abilities or become totally dependent on others. In assisted suicide, a friend or doctor supplies the patient with the means to end his or her life, for example, a large number of sleeping pills.

Mercy killing

In the case of euthanasia, or 'mercy killing', people have already become too ill to kill themselves. A doctor would have to act for them.

He or she might act passively by stopping treatment, such as turning off a life-support machine. Alternatively, he or she may actively end the patient's life, for example, by injecting a poisonous drug.

Today, euthanasia is legal only in Oregon, USA and in Holland. There are concerns about it because people may say they want to die, but their sickness may have made them unable to think clearly. Euthanasia causes problems for doctors, whose job is to preserve life but also to stop suffering. Some have broken the law and helped terminally ill patients to die.

Caring for and befriending terminally ill people can help them to make the most of their last days, months or years.

I believe often that death is good medical treatment, because it can achieve what all today's medical advances and technology cannot achieve – and that is to stop the suffering of the patient.

(Christiaan Barnard – South African surgeon who carried out the world's first heart transplant)

Dr Death

Probably the most famous person linked with euthanasia is the American Dr Jack Kevorkian (pictured above right), often called Dr Death. He devised a machine called the *thanatron* (Greek for 'death machine'). It has switches to allow a patient to inject him or herself with lethal drugs. Dr Kevorkian said his machine made death 'dignified, humane and painless and the patient can do it in the comfort of their own home at any time they want.' When the authorities stopped him from buying the necessary drugs, he helped his patients to kill themselves with poisonous carbon monoxide from car exhaust gases. After assisting around 130 people to end their lives, Dr Kevorkian was jailed for murder in April 1999.

Failed suicide attempts

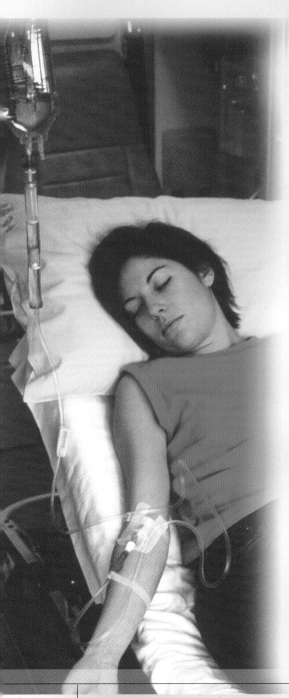

Experts believe that for every suicide there may be up to 100 failed attempts. However, people who have survived a suicide attempt will not necessarily walk away unharmed. One of the biggest problems is with **tylenol/paracetamol**. More than 50 per cent of young women who attempt suicide do so by taking an overdose of these painkillers. Within a short time, they may change their minds and be glad to find they are still alive. However, they often do not know that the drug takes four hours to be absorbed by their body.

If they get to hospital quickly, doctors may make them eat a mix of gooey black charcoal to remove the poison. Unlike in the movies, stomach pumping, in which a hose is forced into the stomach and the contents sucked out, is rare. Not only painful, it can also cause death through stomach acid getting into the lungs.

Specialist treatment

If the overdose took place much more than four hours before, patients are hooked up to an **intravenous drip** for 32 hours, to help flush out the poison. They will later need specialist treatment. Tylenol/paracetamol is toxic to the liver so they may even need a liver transplant.

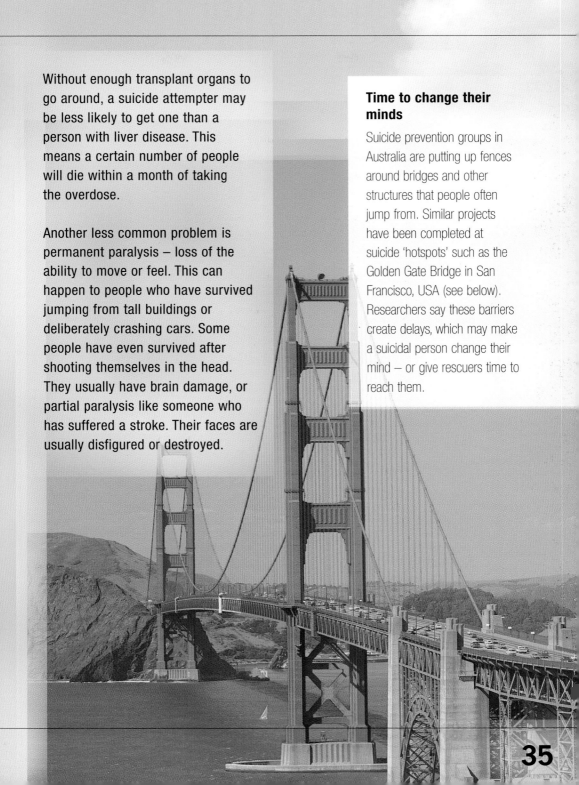

Without enough transplant organs to go around, a suicide attempter may be less likely to get one than a person with liver disease. This means a certain number of people will die within a month of taking the overdose.

Another less common problem is permanent paralysis – loss of the ability to move or feel. This can happen to people who have survived jumping from tall buildings or deliberately crashing cars. Some people have even survived after shooting themselves in the head. They usually have brain damage, or partial paralysis like someone who has suffered a stroke. Their faces are usually disfigured or destroyed.

Time to change their minds

Suicide prevention groups in Australia are putting up fences around bridges and other structures that people often jump from. Similar projects have been completed at suicide 'hotspots' such as the Golden Gate Bridge in San Francisco, USA (see below). Researchers say these barriers create delays, which may make a suicidal person change their mind – or give rescuers time to reach them.

Surviving an attempt

However miserable things can seem for a person who is suicidal or has just survived a suicide attempt, it is important to remember that life can get better. At the very least it may, with time, become more bearable. Many famous people have tried to commit suicide, but have gone on to achieve great things in life. Mark Twain, creator of stories about Tom Sawyer and Huckleberry Finn, once put a loaded revolver to his head but could not bring himself to pull the trigger. Some survivors go on to become counsellors, helping other young people who are going through similar problems.

Help to heal

Post-traumatic stress disorder is common among suicide survivors, and they need counselling to help deal with this. They might suffer either from

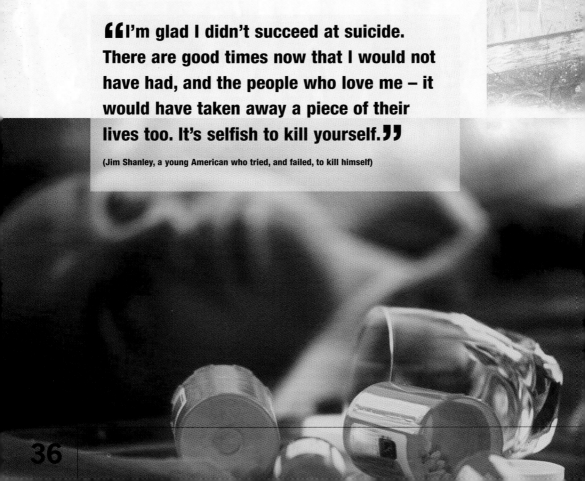

"I'm glad I didn't succeed at suicide. There are good times now that I would not have had, and the people who love me – it would have taken away a piece of their lives too. It's selfish to kill yourself."

(Jim Shanley, a young American who tried, and failed, to kill himself)

Suicide survivors may be teased by those who do not understand what drove them to it.

frightening memories or 'flashbacks' of the attempt, or lose their memory of it altogether. They may feel anxious and guilty. Survivors may not want to talk about what happened, but this does not mean they have got over it. Recovery takes time, so people should not be told to 'pull themselves together' or that it is 'all in the past'.

Suicide stigma

People who have tried to commit suicide will probably be very depressed. They are more likely than the population at large to try to kill themselves again, especially in the first three months after an attempt. The danger may not fully pass for some years. There is still **stigma** about suicide. Survivors often find their friends or family do not know how to cope with what has happened. They may react with anger, or may heap all the blame on themselves. Others may avoid survivors because they do not know what to say. They may pretend it has not happened and refuse to talk about it.

The people left behind

Often, parents and families are forgotten after a young person's suicide or suicide attempt. Yet they too can suffer from **post-traumatic stress disorder**. This may be worse if they were the one to find the body, were with the person as they died or watched **paramedics** trying to revive him or her. Family members will often have to identify the corpse in a hospital morgue, the storage room for dead bodies. They may even have to cut down the body or clean up the place where the person killed him or herself. Many methods of suicide badly damage the body and are horribly messy.

In the weeks, months and years after the suicide, loved ones try to come to terms with strong emotions such as shock, confusion and anger. Their friends and neighbours may not know what to say, or may even blame the family for what happened. Close friends or family members may fall into deep **depression** and attempt suicide themselves. Professional counselling can be helpful for them.

Understanding why

One of the hardest things for those left behind is trying to understand why the teenager committed suicide.

Only around 15 per cent of teenage suicides leave a note. Unless the person wrote down their feelings in a diary there may never be any way of knowing why he or she took their own life. Unlike in cases of natural death, such as from illness, the parents and family often find they cannot fully get over a suicide. They will be left wondering if there was anything they could have done to prevent it.

Sometimes families who have lost a young person to suicide find it helps to design the headstone, or plant a memorial tree. They might make a web page dedicated to the child or keep a diary about their feelings.

❝You spend your whole time trying to understand why he chose death instead of life, whether we were at all to blame, and why he did not tell his father or me – who would have given our own lives to save him had we only known.❞

(Anne Parry, a science teacher whose son killed himself in 1994)

Myths about suicide

Although we are slowly learning more about suicide, it is still a subject often surrounded by lies, confusion and secrecy. This can be dangerous, because it can mean a person's suicidal feelings may not be recognized or taken seriously until it is too late.

It is very important, therefore, to separate the facts about suicide from the myths.

Myth: People who threaten to commit suicide do not try to kill themselves.

Fact: Eight out of ten people who commit suicide have said they feel like dying.

Myth: People who kill themselves really want to die.

Fact: Most suicidal people are not sure whether they want to live or die. Suicide is often a cry for help during a crisis.

Myth: Once the **depression** seems to be lifting, the danger is past.

Fact: This can be the most dangerous stage. If something goes wrong now it can make the person feel even worse. Their apparent calm may be due to relief after finally deciding on suicide.

Myth: If someone talks about suicide, it is important to get his or her mind off it and change the subject.

Fact: By talking openly with him or her, a friend will make the suicidal person feel they are being taken seriously. If the friend finds out the person has a definite plan for the suicide, it is important to get help quickly.

Myth: Someone who has tried to kill himself or herself will not do it again.

Fact: At least 30 per cent of teenage suicides have made a previous attempt.

Myth: Threatening suicide is a type of emotional blackmail, which should be ignored or punished.

Fact: All suicide threats should be taken seriously.

Myth: Suicide sometimes comes 'out of the blue'.

Fact: No one ends their life for no reason, although the warning signs may be hard to recognize.

Myth: If someone swears a friend to secrecy about a suicide plan, that person must not tell anyone about it.

Fact: Someone who helps another person to kill him or herself is not a good friend.

Myth: If the suicidal person is in counselling or therapy, he or she is safe.

Fact: Around 15 per cent of teenagers who commit suicide are undergoing treatment at the time of their death.

[Male] Doctor: 'You're not even old enough to know how bad life gets.'
Cecilia: 'You've never been a thirteen-year-old girl.'

(From the film *The Virgin Suicides*, about five young sisters who committed suicide in the 1970s)

Tackling teenage suicide

The United Nations (UN), World Health Organization and governments in most Western countries recognize youth suicide as a major problem. The UN has suggested governments should set up programmes to deal with all the factors linked to suicide, such as mental illnesses, youth unemployment, child abuse, drugs and alcoholism. However, in developing countries it is often still a taboo issue that is not discussed.

In many schools in the West, teachers are trained to identify pupils who appear unhappy. Students are taught problem-solving and confidence-boosting skills. Most schools also have programmes to crack down on bullying. There are also efforts to reduce suicide in prisons. Young inmates are helped by a **psychiatrist** and put on suicide watch if thought to be at risk. They are checked hourly during the night.

Suicide prevention

In the United States, the Surgeon General outlined the country's first-ever national strategy for suicide prevention in May 2001. A key issue involves training doctors and nurses to recognize the signs of **depression** and mental illness among young people earlier. Then they can offer them treatment before their problems become severe.

Australia's US$20 million youth suicide prevention strategy, set up in 1995, partly focuses on teaching families better parenting skills. New Zealand's strategy, 'In Our Hands', was launched in 1998. It hopes to limit access to the means of committing suicide, such as guns, and to offer more support to families with at-risk children.

In the United Kingdom, the government aims to reduce the suicide rate by one-fifth by 2010, and has set up special counselling lines for young men in areas of high male unemployment. In Ireland, a special task force was set up in 1995 to raise public awareness of the factors involved in suicide.

Young offenders need a wide range of activities to keep them fit, active and mentally alert to avoid sinking into depression while in detention.

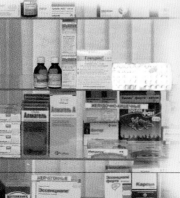

Removing the poisons

Many studies have shown that removing access to the means of suicide has led to a big fall in the overall suicide rate. For example, the poisons were removed from oven gas in the 1960s. **Catalytic converters** make exhaust gases less toxic in cars. In the UK, **tylenol/paracetamol** is sold only in packs of sixteen. This is thought to reduce the risk, but it is important to remember that this is an extremely dangerous drug if mis-used.

What to do

Health professionals look for particular signs in someone they think might be suicidal. Spotting these is often difficult. However, some warning behaviour includes saying things such as: 'I won't be a problem for you much longer' or 'It's no use'. The person may say 'I won't see you again', or complain of feeling 'rotten inside'.

People might start to prepare for the suicide by giving away precious possessions or cleaning their bedroom. Their eating and sleeping habits may change or they may stay away from friends and family. They might give up activities they once enjoyed, such as sports, music or going to the cinema.

On the other hand, people who are planning suicide could seem unusually happy, panicky or agitated. They might take a lot of risks, such as driving too fast. They might sleep around or rebel against their parents or teachers. Other risk signs include suffering from **hallucinations**, or developing obsessions about particular things, such as hand washing or losing weight.

Caring for the suicidal

If a person seems likely to attempt suicide soon, experts advise the following:
- Do not leave them alone. Suicidal people may ask their parents, brothers or sisters to leave the house so they can carry out the suicide.
- Try to keep them talking until the crisis has passed.
- Get help, by calling for an ambulance, the police or a trusted adult.

If a person has survived a suicide attempt, it is important to do these things:
- Keep a careful eye on him or her, but do not be overprotective.
- Do not force the person to talk about the suicide attempt. Only discuss it if they bring it up.
- Get back to the regular family routine as soon as possible.
- Remove any dangerous substances or weapons, such as guns, rope, poisons and medicines. The risk of suicide is much lower if the means of suicide are removed. For example, in the USA, where many people keep guns at home, around 60 per cent of suicide victims shoot themselves. There are hardly any such deaths in the UK, where guns are illegal.
- Get professional help and advice. It is important to face problems and not sweep them under the carpet.

Some people at risk of suicide might not appear to be depressed at all. In fact they might seem very energetic and the 'life and soul of the party'.

Legal matters

Suicide is no longer illegal in any Western country. The major legal issue therefore concerns **euthanasia** – stopping a sick person's treatment, or injecting them with a drug to make them die. This includes assisted suicide – giving a sick person the means to kill themselves, for example a large amount of drugs. Euthanasia is illegal nearly everywhere, and can result in a murder charge and a possible life sentence in prison. Assisted suicide also often carries a heavy penalty, although less severe than for euthanasia cases.

However, courts often treat people who have assisted a suicide less harshly than cold-blooded murderers. They may be sympathetic if it is clear the person was suffering unbearable pain and really wanted to end his or her life. In most places, passive euthanasia is legal. Patients can choose to refuse treatment that is keeping them alive.

Living wills

Some people make living wills, which may be written or recorded on a video or an audio tape. They state their wish for passive euthanasia if they are unable to give permission for it, for example, if they have fallen into a coma. If a person has made a living will, the doctor who helps the patient to die is less likely to be prosecuted.

The only country where active euthanasia is legal is the Netherlands. In the United States, the state of Oregon passed a 'Death with Dignity Act' in 1994, which allows assisted suicide if death is likely within six months. However, attempts to pass similar laws in Michigan (1998), California (2000) and Maine (2000) all failed. In Australia, Northern Territory State passed a bill to allow euthanasia in 1996, but this was overturned by the National Parliament in 1997.

Legal euthanasia

Doctors in the Netherlands have been allowed to give overdoses of drugs to people with a 'concrete expectancy of death' since 2000. However, the regulations are strict to make sure the law is not abused. Doctors may also carry out euthanasia on **terminally ill** children above the age of twelve, although those under sixteen must get their parents' permission. Neighbouring Belgium looks likely to legalize euthanasia in the near future too.

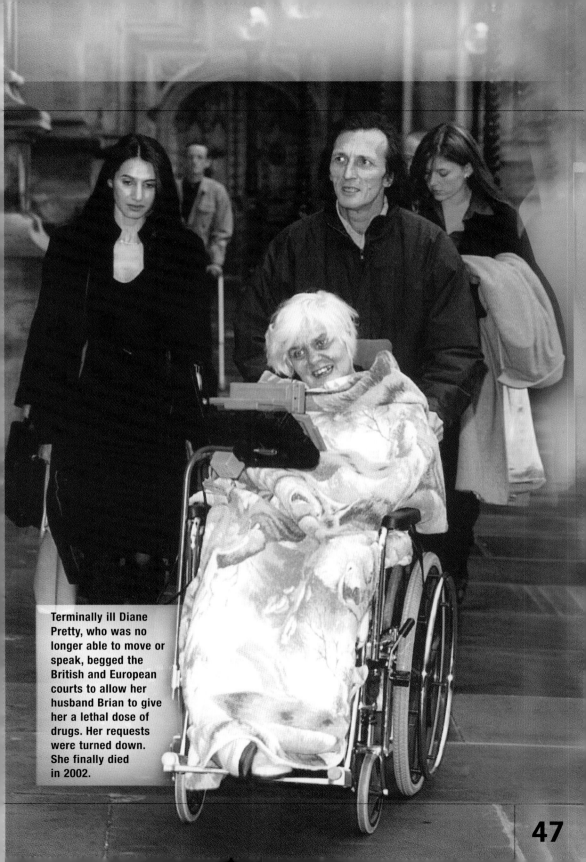

Terminally ill Diane Pretty, who was no longer able to move or speak, begged the British and European courts to allow her husband Brian to give her a lethal dose of drugs. Her requests were turned down. She finally died in 2002.

Treatment and counselling

Many organizations exist to help suicidal people find an alternative to ending their lives. People who get help before they make a suicide attempt are likely to recover better and quicker than those who never tell anyone about how they feel until after they have tried to kill themselves.

However, some suicidal teenagers may feel frightened or embarrassed about seeking professional help. They may be drug users or in trouble with the law, or mistakenly think that counselling is only for people who are 'crazy'. There is no shame in seeking help. Being depressed is fairly common and definitely does not mean a person is mad.

Talking

It may seem simple, but talking is one of the best ways of dealing with **depression** and suicidal feelings. People who can open up and talk about the bad things going on in their lives often find it easier to work out a way of solving their problems. People who feel hopeless and keep everything bottled up may become more and more convinced there is no solution.

Many depressed people feel that the people around them do not understand their problems, or will not listen. However, there are dozens of professional groups who will listen in confidence. They will not tell anybody, although they may contact the emergency services if they think the person is going to hurt him or herself or someone else. Many counsellors have had similar problems themselves. They will not be angry if a person admits to feeling suicidal and will take his or her problems seriously.

Helplines

Helplines are available 24 hours a day to help people who are going through a crisis. As the conversations are anonymous, helplines are often used by people who are not yet ready to talk to a doctor or counsellor.

Many organizations, such as Samaritans and Befrienders, now have email counselling services, which are very popular with young people. Teenagers may feel happier getting help via the internet rather than face-to-face. The Samaritans' website even has a button that can be clicked to make the Samaritans' logo disappear. This means that in a public place, nobody else will realize the person is using a counselling service.

Treatment and counselling

Schools

Many schools in the USA and Australia have suicide prevention programmes. Schools may also have special counsellors, who are trained to help young people with their problems. If not, a trusted teacher can usually offer a sympathetic ear, or give advice about how to find professional help.

Religious leaders

Religious leaders, such as priests, rabbis and imams, can help too. They may be able to give a more spiritual view of how to overcome problems. For some people, religious faith can help a person to see life's problems as part of a 'bigger picture', making some kind of sense of his or her difficulties.

Psychotherapy

Some people find professional **psychotherapy** is the most helpful way to sort out their suicidal feelings. The therapist talks to the person about what is making him or her depressed and how to cope with the difficulties of daily life. The person learns how to fight off **depression** if it returns.

Drug treatment

A doctor may treat a suicidal person with anti-depressant drugs as well as referring him or her for professional therapy. The drugs can give a person some 'breathing space' to decide how to tackle his or her problems. Modern anti-depressants, such as Prozac, are not habit-forming. But they are powerful drugs that affect the brain's chemistry. There may be some side-effects, usually when a person starts to take them. These may include sickness, dizziness, insomnia (inability to sleep) and the feeling of living in a dream. More serious and rare conditions, such as **manic depression** and **schizophrenia**, can also be treated with drugs. The earlier people get treatment, the less likely they are to commit suicide.

Drug users' clinics

Doctors or therapists may also refer people to drug users' clinics. There they will receive help in kicking their drink or drug habit, which might have played a large role in their depression or suicidal feelings. However, this treatment will not work unless the person really wants to give up the habit. He or she will receive counselling and gradually lowered doses of replacement drugs. It is not necessary to go 'cold turkey' and give up the drugs straight away.

Emergency services

In extreme cases, the police can restrain people to stop them from killing themselves. The emergency services, such as ambulance workers and **paramedics**, will resuscitate (revive) people. They will take them to hospital, where doctors will do everything to keep them alive. After treatment, **psychiatrists** will keep an eye on them until it is safe for them to go home. Very agitated people may be kept sedated – put on drugs to keep them calm.

Information and advice

The following organizations and websites can offer information and support for people who are depressed and suicidal, and for their friends and families. Many of them give advice on how to get through some crisis areas in teenage life, such as school exams.

A useful site is **Befrienders International** at www.befrienders.org. It has links to 1700 crisis centres and helplines worldwide. There are 31,000 volunteers working in 41 countries, providing 24-hour telephone and confidential email counselling.

A bullying-related site is: www.teasingvictims.com

A good site about depression is: www.belljar.co.uk

Contacts in the UK

Childline
Freepost 1111, London NW1 0BR
Bullying hotline: Tel: 0800 1111
www.childline.org.uk

Depression Alliance
35 Westminster Bridge Road, London SE1 7JB
Tel: 020 76330557
www.depressionalliance.org

Papyrus (families of suicide victims)
Rossendale GH, Union Road, Rawtenstall,
Lancashire BB4 6NE
Tel: 01706 214449 www.papyrus-uk.org

Samaritans
The Upper Mill, Kingston Road, Ewell,
Surrey KT17 2AF
Helpline Tel: 08457 909090
www.samaritans.org.uk

Young Minds Parents' Information Service
102–108 Clerkenwell Road, London
EC1M 5SA
Tel: 0800 0182138 www.youngminds.org.uk

Contacts in the USA

National Adolescent Suicide Hotline
Tel: (800) 6214000

National Child Abuse Hotline
(800) 4-A-CHILD, (1 800 422 4453)

National Drug and Alcohol Treatment Hotline
Tel: (800) 662-HELP (1 800 662 4357)

National Youth Crisis Hotline
Tel: (800) HIT-HOME (1 800 448 4663)

Runaway Hotline
(800) 231 6946.

Suicide Hotline
1 888 333 2377

A good information site for suicidal people, survivors and families is the **American Association of Suicidology**, 4201 Connecticut Ave NW, Suite 408, Washington DC 20008 Tel: (202) 237 2280 www.suicidology.org

Contacts in Australia

Kids' Helpline
PO Box 376, Red Hill, QLD 4059
Tel: 1800 55 1800 www.kidshelp.com.au

Lifelink Samaritans (Tasmania)
PO Box 228, Launceston, Tasmania 7250
Tel: 03 63 313355

Samaritans
Tel: 1 800 198313

Contacts in Canada

Crisis Intervention Center
Tel: 1 888 757 7766
www.kidshelp.sympatico.ca

Kids Helpline
Tel: 1 800 668 6868

Suicide Information and Education Center
No.201, 1615–10th Ave SW, Calgary, Alberta T3C 0J7 www.suicideinfo.ca
This organization provides information, education, great links and numbers for many local crisis and counselling centres.

Contacts in New Zealand

Samaritans (Wellington)
Tel: 04 473-9739

Contacts in Ireland

Childline Freephone
Tel: 1800 666666

National Suicide Bereavement Support Network Community Centre, Main St, Killeagh, Co. Cork
Tel: 024 95561

Samaritans
112 Marlborough St, Dublin 1
Tel: 01 872 7700

Schizophrenia Ireland
38 Blessington St, Dublin 7 Tel: 01 860 1620 www.sirl.ie

Further reading

His Bright Light by Danielle Steel; Bantam Press, 1998. The true story of the son of novelist Danielle Steel. A manic depression sufferer, he first considered suicide at 13 and finally killed himself at 19.

Healing After the Suicide of a Loved One by Ann Smolin and John Guinan; Simon and Schuster, 1993

A Parent's Guide for Suicidal and Depressed Teens: Help for Recognizing if a Child is in Crisis and What to Do About It by Kate Williams; Hazelden Information and Educational Services, 1995

Need to Know: Depression by Claire Wallerstein; Heinemann, 2003

Night Falls Fast: Understanding Suicide by Kay Redfield Jamison; Picador, 2000

Depression: The Way Out of Your Prison by Dorothy Rowe; Routledge, 1996

Glossary

Aborigine
original people of Australia, who were living there before European settlers arrived

abortion
operation carried out to end a pregnancy

anorexic
a person suffering from anorexia nervosa, a mental illness. Sufferers become obsessed with their body weight and starve themselves, often to the point of death.

bipolar affective disorder
also known as manic depression. People have periods of severe depression and periods of heightened energy, excitement and happiness (mania).

bulimia
an eating disorder – sufferers often gorge themselves on huge amounts of food and then make themselves vomit or take laxatives to get rid of the food

bullycide
suicide committed as a result of being bullied

catalytic converter
attachment in a car which uses chemicals to make the car's exhaust fumes less toxic

catatonic
condition suffered by some patients with schizophrenia, in which they become rigid and cannot move

cult
a group, usually religious, that follows a strange or extreme belief system, often led by one powerful leader

deliberate self-harm
when someone hurts themselves on purpose. They may cut themselves because it gives them a sense of relief at a stressful time.

delusion
a fixed, but false, belief. Schizophrenia sufferers often have delusions, for example that a particular person is spying on them.

depression
a medical condition in which a person feels very miserable over a long period of time

disembowel
to remove the innards, or guts, from a person or animal

DNA
genetic material inside the cells of all living things

euthanasia
a type of assisted suicide, in which a terminally ill person is helped to die

genetic
relating to genes. Genes pass on characteristics from parents to children such as eye colour, height or the likelihood of developing certain diseases.

gene therapy
a new type of medicine in the early stages of development. In the future, scientists hope that faulty genes, such as those that cause certain diseases, could be 'switched off'.

hallucination
seeing things or hearing noises that are not real

hara-kiri
a type of honourable suicide in 16th-century Japan: the person cut open his stomach with a special sword to remove the intestines, and then a friend chopped off his head

hunter-gatherer societies
groups of people who live mostly by hunting and fishing, and collecting wild food

hyperactive
extremely energetic, much more than normal

indigenous
original, or native, people in countries such as the USA, Canada, Australia and New Zealand, who were living there before European settlers arrived

industrialized countries
rich, developed countries, such as the USA, Australia, Japan or European countries, with economies based on high-tech manufacturing rather than farming

intravenous drip
usually a sugar-salt solution that passes directly into a vein through a needle

kamikaze
the name of Japanese pilots in the Second World War, who crashed their planes into enemy targets, killing themselves in the process

laxative
drug which relaxes the muscles of the bowels, allowing the body to get rid of waste food before it has been fully absorbed

manic depression – see bipolar affective disorder

Maoris
native people of New Zealand

paramedic
type of medical officer; paramedics often arrive in ambulances, and are usually the first on the scene in an emergency

parasuicide
an act that appears to be an attempted suicide but was probably not intended to be successful

phototherapy
treatment with bright ultra-violet light lamps to treat seasonal affective disorder (SAD)

post-traumatic stress disorder
a condition often suffered by people following a very stressful or traumatic event, such as a suicide attempt

psychiatrist
a type of doctor who specializes in mental illnesses

psychosis
symptoms typical of schizophrenia patients, such as delusions, hallucinations and mental confusion

psychotherapy
a 'talking cure' through which people are helped to understand what led to their depression

schizophrenia
a mental illness caused by a chemical imbalance in the brain, in which a person suffers from psychosis and has an increased risk of suicide

seasonal affective disorder (SAD)
a type of depression caused by a lack of the ultra-violet light found in sunlight

serotonin
a chemical in the brain which, among other functions, controls mood

sociologist
a person who studies how human society works

stigma
shame or disgrace linked to a certain person or subject, usually through ignorance

terminally ill
suffering from an illness that cannot be cured and will lead to death

tylenol/parecetamol medicine often used as a painkiller or to bring down fever

unipolar affective disorder the medical name for depression – see depression

Index

Titles in the *Need to Know* series include:

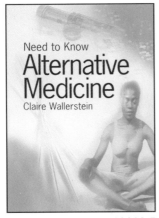

Need to Know
Alternative Medicine
Claire Wallerstein

Hardback   0 431 09808 5

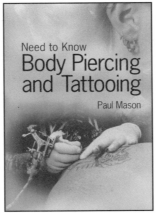

Need to Know
Body Piercing and Tattooing
Paul Mason

Hardback   0 431 09818 2

Need to Know
Depression
Claire Wallerstein

Hardback   0 431 09809 3

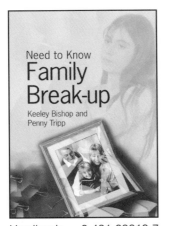

Need to Know
Family Break-up
Keeley Bishop and Penny Tripp

Hardback   0 431 09810 7

Need to Know
Gambling
Michael Smeaton and Paul Bellringer

Hardback   0 431 09819 0

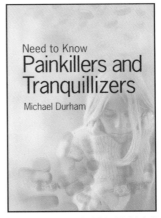

Need to Know
Painkillers and Tranquillizers
Michael Durham

Hardback   0 431 09811 5

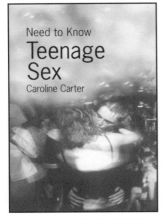

Need to Know
Teenage Sex
Caroline Carter

Hardback   0 431 09821 2

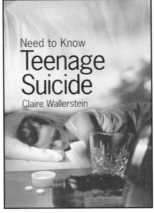

Need to Know
Teenage Suicide
Claire Wallerstein

Hardback   0 431 09820 4

Find out about the other titles in this series on our website www.heinemann.co.uk/library